GRADUATING

GIRLHOOD

GRADUATING GIRLHOOD

A Teenage Girl's Guide to Success in Relationships & Life

Denise K. Evans

A Life-Enhancing Publication

Copyright © 2003 Denise Evans

All rights reserved.

Except for brief quotations or excerpts for purposes of critical review, no part of this book may be reproduced in any manner without the written permission of the publisher.

ISBN 0-9722720-0-3
Library of Congress Control Number: 2002092914

Manufactured in the United States of America

Life-Enhancing Publishing
P.O. Box 681427, Riverside, Missouri 64168

This book is dedicated to God . . .

With whom
ALL things are possible!

Table of Contents

Introduction
xi

~1~
Me, Myself & I
(Most important element to having good relationships)
1

~2~
Who Does She Think She Is?!?
(Relationships with other girls)
23

~3~
Where do Teenage Boys come from?
(Relationships with boys)
39

~4~
Don't Go With the Flow!
(Peer pressure & popularity)
53

GRADUATING GIRLHOOD

~5~
They Just Don't Understand
(Relationships with parents & other adults)
63

~6~
"If Only My_____Were_____"
(Body Image)
75

~7~
If You Aim at Nothing,
You'll Hit It Every Time!
(Determine your gifts, set some goals)
93

~8~
If You're Really Lucky,
You will Be Successful . . . NOT!
(Elements of effective goal setting—

luck is not one of them)
103

~9~
GIRL POWER!
(Final words of wisdom)
115

Acknowledgments

It is with utmost gratitude that I acknowledge and thank Jose, Ronda and my parents for being my inner circle of love and support.

GRADUATING GIRLHOOD became reality with the personal and/or professional involvement of many talented people. In that regard, I would also like to thank:

Cathy Newton, Kim Folsom, Susan Hoskins, Debra Hirsch, Kolette Schneider, Jami Helpting, Denise Whithorne, David Wurster, Dan Poynter and Mark Ortman.

x

Introduction

OK, so life has given you an assignment: You are a teenage girl who has to develop, evolve and mature into a happy and successful woman. There is no turning back now. The wheels of life are in motion. You are on the road to becoming an adult, like it or not!

Perhaps you do like the idea. Perhaps you are excited and hopeful and ready to take on the future. Or maybe the assignment has taken you by surprise. "Yesterday I was playing with Barbie and riding my bike, and today I have to make decisions about . . . WHAT?!" (Sex, college, career, relationships!)

GRADUATING GIRLHOOD

I've been there. And the adult women you know have been there, too. It is not easy. And I'm going to let you in on a little secret: The changes, the choices and sometimes confusion don't end with your teens. I know it doesn't seem possible, but you will be growing, changing and experiencing many new things throughout most of your 20s, too. The process just STARTS now, in your teens. To add to the confusion are the many mixed messages bombarding you. Movies, music videos and teen magazines put thoughts in your head. They make you feel like you should look, dress and act a certain way.

Who can you turn to for advice or direction? Television talk shows mostly address adult situations or extreme situations for teens. Teen magazines promote glamour, fashion, hairstyles and boys as what it's all about. And your friends, although you love them, are going through much of the same stuff that you are. You can share your concerns with them, but you want someone to talk to who's been there. Even if you are fortunate enough to have par-

Introduction

ents who are attentive and want to be there for you, it is still often difficult to take advice from them. You feel that they still see you as a "kid," or like you used to be, when you feel so different now.

So where does all this leave you? What's a girl to do? This book is written especially for you! In the following nine chapters, you will find straight talk and insights on issues that you're facing. I hope you will find the information interesting, thought-provoking and most of all . . . helpful!

Creating

Healthy

Relationships

~1~

Me, Myself & I

As you graduate girlhood, and travel through adolescence and into womanhood, relationships will be a source of your happiest moments in life and, unfortunately, sometimes your most painful.

The next few years are the time in your life when relationships and friendships are changing and becoming more important to you. Your relationships with boys are changing, and your relationships with adults are changing. It is natural to worry about what other people think of you, to try to fit in with your peers, and to want boys to notice you.

GRADUATING GIRLHOOD

Getting a boyfriend is probably important to you now. Keeping your parents happy (or at least off your back) is important. So we are going to begin by discussing this key area of development. This chapter begins our look into the complicated but important subject of relationships.

Relationships are a big part of every woman's life. They are becoming a more significant part of your life as you meet new people in middle school, in high school, in college, and at work. As women, we get a sense of joy, fulfillment, meaning, and esteem from our relationships. I'm not just talking about from our relationships with the opposite sex. We have important relationships with our girlfriends, our parents, our siblings, other family members, our classmates, our teachers, our co-workers, and our employers.

Because relationships are so important to us, our ability to have or not have good ones affects the quality of our lives. You can make straight A's, be homecoming queen or win a million dollars, but if you don't feel good about the relationships in your life, you won't be happy.

It is interesting that relationships make up so much of life and affect so many decisions we make, yet when we become teenagers heading to adulthood, we are not taught basic relationship skills. "Personal Relationships 101" is not offered as a course in school. We are not given directions. We're usually just left to figure things out on our own. The problem is that by the time it takes to get some things figured out, many young women have made irreversible mistakes. Reading this book will give you a good start and help you to avoid common pitfalls that many girls make.

The information shown on television, in the movies and in magazines concerning relationships is confusing. They make it seem like the way you look has something to do with having good relationships, or that a relationship with a boy has to revolve around the physical aspect. Both are not true! So let's talk about a positive way to look at and make sense of the many relationships in your life.

When we think about what components make up a good relationship, we think of things like honesty, trust and communication. These are indeed important, but the most important element that will determine the quality of the relationships you have in your life is . . . the relationship you have with yourself. Please don't read forward until you think about that. The quality of the relationship you have with **yourself** directly affects the quality of the relationships you have with other people.

You might not even realize that you have a relationship with yourself, but you do. Your relationship with yourself is how you *feel* about yourself, how you **talk** to yourself. Do you *feel* like you'll never measure up? Or do you feel like you are just as good as the next person?

How is your relationship with yourself (also referred to as self-esteem)? Have you ever thought about it?

Me, Myself & I

The relationship you have with yourself begins in your thoughts. You talk to yourself in your mind every day. You might say, "I do not talk to myself!" But your mind is thinking thoughts . . . almost constantly. Your brain is always chattering and analyzing things. So, what are you thinking? What kinds of things do you tell yourself? Do you judge yourself in a negative light? Do you think things like "I could never be good at math" or "I am not as good as she is"? Or do you think things like "I am just as good as the next person" and "If I try hard enough, I can achieve anything I set my mind to"?

Your relationship with yourself begins with your thoughts, so it is time to start paying attention to them. You might be amazed by what you notice. If you find yourself thinking mostly negative thoughts, try to replace those ideas with something better.

You don't have to lie to yourself and say, for example, "I have the most perfect body and I should be a supermodel!" But instead of saying "I am a fat pig and I'll never have a boyfriend," you can say,

"I'm shorter than I'd like to be, but my legs look good, and I am grateful to be healthy and I am good at <u>gymnastic</u>(music, sports, art). Doesn't that make you feel better? Keeping perspective is crucial.

For every negative thing you think about yourself, if you try, you can also find a positive thing. The point is that you first have to notice the negative self-talk, then make the effort to find something positive. Consciously thinking and saying a positive statement to yourself is called an affirmation. It helps in times of stress and doubt to repeat a positive statement throughout the day. Affirmations help cancel out negative feelings and convince the insecure part of yourself that you are in control!

An affirmation is never negative. Instead of saying "I can't eat candy and drink soda for breakfast," you say, "I choose to eat healthy food in the morning to fuel my busy day."

◇◇◇◇◇◇

At the end of each chapter in this book, you will find the beginning of two affirmations that relate to the topic you just read about. It'll be up to you to personalize the affirming sentences by completing them with words that apply to you. And then it is up to you to think about what you've written and repeat the positive phrase throughout your day!

Paying attention to your thoughts and working on your relationship with yourself is not something you will outgrow. You'll never get to a place where everything feels perfect all the time. Everyone has good days and bad days. Some days you will feel confident about things in your life, and other days you'll feel not so confident. There are also specific areas of your life that you may struggle with. You may feel good about your ability to make good grades, but not so good about your hair. It is normal to have some insecurities. You worry, "Am I pretty enough? Does this zit show up from across the room? Is my body OK?" etc.

Normal insecure thoughts like that are not obsessive to a person who has a good relationship with herself. Those thoughts come to mind for a few minutes, but then you go about your day. Remember this: There is always someone out there who is better off than you and someone who is worse off than you. There is someone with more zits today, and someone with fewer zits than you today!

That's a good way to keep perspective and on track. If you find that you are beating up on yourself about something, *any* issue, just tell yourself that there is someone out there better off than you and someone worse off than you. Think of the issue you are struggling with (your hair, body, clothes, money, education, relationship with your parents) and think of people who have it better and who have it worse than you do.

It puts those things in perspective immediately. When you think about someone who is *worse* off than you, it helps you feel grateful for what you do have. And when you realize that someone, somewhere is *better* off than you, you recognize

Me, Myself & I

that life is not perfect for that person just because this one thing is better.

The way you think has a big impact on the way you feel about yourself. Feeling good or bad about yourself comes across, and other people respond to that.

In addition to your thoughts, the choices that you make are another indicator of the relationship that you have with yourself. Do you make choices based on what other people think? Do you make choices because it's what other people want you to do? Or do you make choices based on what's best for **YOU**? Are your choices ones that are going to help you achieve your goals and get you where you want to be? Do you care for and honor yourself, or do you treat others better?

You are at an age when you are making REALLY BIG choices—like what classes to take in school; whether or not to go to college; whether or not to have sex, smoke or drink alcohol. These are very big decisions that you will be making if you haven't already. All of them have huge consequences. You may not realize it, but the choices you make today will have a dramatic impact on your future. Will you be prepared for college because you took the right courses in school? Will you be confident later in life when you meet the man you're going to marry because you don't have any sexually transmitted diseases from having sex as a teenager? Will you feel unhealthy and out of breath when you go up a flight of stairs because you smoke?

These may not sound like important benefits to you now, but talk to someone who is dealing with these issues and you will realize how tremendously rewarding it is to take the time to think about the choices you make and the consequences that come with them.

If you have a good relationship with yourself, it shows because you don't mistreat yourself by participating in risky behavior that can hurt you . . . like smoking, drugs and sex. And you do not allow others to mistreat you.

On the other hand, if you do not have a good relationship with yourself, you are willing to try risky behavior. You'll try anything that might make you temporarily feel better and mask who you really are and how you really feel. You might try drugs or alcohol to fit in or look cool, or because you think it will take away the negative feelings you have about yourself.

Why don't these substances really work to make you feel better? Because in numbing the pain or insecurity, they also numb your ability to feel true joy and happiness. Drugs and alcohol impair your judgment so you talk and behave in ways that you are not proud of later, causing you to feel even worse than before. Not to mention that these substances are illegal, addictive, expensive, and destructive to your life and everyone around you.

Think about a recent choice you made. Did that choice reflect who you really are or who you want to be, or did that choice make life even more confusing for you?

Have you heard the statement "Be true to yourself"? That sounds great! We would all like to do that, but how? What does it mean to be true to yourself?

Well, the very first thing you have to do to be true to yourself is know yourself. If you don't really know who you are and what you believe in and what you want, how can you be true to yourself? There are three specific things you can do to help you get to know yourself better that will enable you to be true to yourself: Spend time alone, keep a diary, and trust your instincts.

Getting to know your self is an ongoing journey in life. A great way to get started is to get in the habit of spending some time alone. If you think about it, how much time do you spend alone? I mean without the TV, without the radio, without being on the phone or computer. How much time do you spend just by yourself, thinking about things going on in your life, thinking about the people, the choices and the decisions you have to make? We can stay so distracted by TV, magazines, music, and what our friends are telling us, that we do not even realize what our own opinions really are; we just buy in to what everyone else is saying.

Spending some quiet time with ourselves is a crucial part of knowing who we really are and what we really want for ourselves. It may feel uncomfortable at first, but keep making the effort. Soon you will look forward to your private time without distractions.

It can be challenging, but try to make sure you are getting some quality time alone every week to think about things going on in your life. With all the stress of being a teenager and living in the 21st century, it is easy to feel over whelmed. This is a great way to get focused. It is an important habit to start now.

Another way to get to know yourself is by keeping a diary. Having a private place to write your thoughts and feelings is an invaluable way of getting in touch with yourself. Your diary or journal doesn't have to be a fancy, formal book. Decorate a spiral notebook and you have a diary!

You do not have to write in your diary or journal every day. Certainly writing things like "went to school," "had pizza for lunch" and "Joey said 'hi' to me in the hall" are not as beneficial as writing your thoughts and feelings. You have all kinds of important things going on and decisions to make, so write about them! Your diary is a place to write down feelings, frustrations and fears that you have.

There is something about actually writing out what's on your mind that often makes you feel better. For one thing, it gets whatever you're writing about "off your chest." Another thing is that while your head is telling your hand what to write, your heart will sometimes reveal something else. It's as if you gain a new or different perspective. Some situations or solutions can become more clear.

Me, Myself & I

Lots of men and women keep a journal throughout their whole lives. Having a personal place to write is a great way to get to know yourself and to stay in touch with yourself as you change throughout the years. You can look back later at what you wrote and see how far you've come!

If you feel uncomfortable about keeping a diary or if you think you don't know what else to write besides what you did that day, try writing a letter (that you won't send, of course) to someone you're mad at. Or write a letter to God expressing your concerns about an issue you're dealing with.

You can try your hand at poetry. Write a poem in your journal about your happiness or your sadness today. It doesn't have to rhyme and it doesn't have to make sense to anyone else. Writing your thoughts in the form of poetry can be a tool for expressing yourself and something fun to practice.

The third way you can be true to yourself is to trust your gut instinct. Have you ever met someone who you were uncomfortable around right away, even though you didn't even know him or her? There was just something about the person that you didn't like. Or have you had the opposite experience of meeting someone whom you did like right away, even though you didn't know him or her? You didn't have a lot of real information about the person, but right away you had a feeling about them. That is your gut instinct, or intuition.

Part of being true to yourself is paying attention to those instincts when you have them and honoring them. That doesn't mean that you get an uncomfortable feeling and go running out of the room! It just means that you notice your initial instinct and allow that to be part of your decision-making process. Before you proceed further with a person or project, you may need some more information. Or if additional negative feelings come up, you can pay even more attention to them because you sort of "knew" anyway.

You can talk to a lot of people who have had the experience of going against their gut instincts, or

Me, Myself & I

maybe even you have made a choice that you somehow "knew" from the beginning wouldn't work out, but you did it anyway. If we do not pay attention to those internal clues, we almost always live to regret it.

Over the long run, these three practices will enable you to have a great relationship with yourself:

- Spend time alone each week.
- Keep a diary.
- Listen to your intuition.

You will realize, as you grow and mature, that you have everything you need to move forward in life and reach your potential. The answers you are

> *The answers you are seeking are very often found within yourself.*

seeking are very often found within yourself. You will realize that YOU are the most qualified person to know and to understand what you need and what is best for you!

As we conclude chapter one and go on to other important relationships in chapters two-five, I hope you now have a better understanding of your relationship with yourself and how making it a positive one ultimately affects the quality of other relationships in your life.

With divorce and breakups happening all the time, perhaps even in your own family, you must realize by now that good relationships are not easy to achieve. Healthy relationships don't just happen, and they don't last without some real effort and understanding.

It takes a lot of women a lot of years to really understand that if they're having bad relationship after bad relationship, they need to step back and take a good look within themselves to see if their connection with who they are on the inside is how it should be. People can only treat you badly more than once, if you allow them to. Once you're an adult, you will have a choice to be in or not to be in any relationship, with anybody.

Affirmations

Complete the following sentences as they apply to you. Then think about what you've written and repeat the positive phrase throughout your day. Try it, I think you'll like it!

I admire myself for
being the best that I can be and doing well in my work

I enjoy spending quiet time with myself because
people won't annoy me and I can do whatever I want to do

~2~

Who Does She Think She Is?!?

Now that we have established a foundation for you concerning the most important part of forming good relationships and where to begin, let's talk about relationships with other people. After all, that's usually what comes to mind when we think about relationships: us interacting with someone else! Right? That's also usually where things get complicated!

It is only in the movies and in fairy tales that two people meet, fall in love and live happily ever after: no complications, just sheer bliss! (We are saving romance and boys for chapter three.) But even with friendships, we don't just meet another girl, have everything in common, never disagree, and never get disappointed in one another. Let's begin by discussing how to have positive relationships with other girls.

Relationships between girls of all ages can be difficult. For some reason, we are often our own worst enemies. Instead of embracing our differences and what makes us special and unique, we use those differences to compare ourselves and to judge one another.

We compare ourselves with pop stars or movie stars and wind up feeling bad because we don't measure up to what they look like or what we think they have. We compare the new girl in school to the way we dress or act, and then we judge or make fun of her for the ways that she is different.

Life is hard. So why do we make it harder on each other when we could be uplifting and encouraging? Have you ever been hurt by another girl's actions or remarks? Or worse, have you ever been the one to say or do something to hurt another girl for no good reason? (People who criticize or act cruel to others are only trying to cover up their own insecurities.) Think about it. Does anything good ever come from expressing negativity toward others?

One topic that always comes up when talking about issues between girls is jealousy. Jealousy is such a negative emotion. It doesn't feel good to be jealous of someone and it doesn't feel good when someone is jealous of you. If you are jealous of another girl, you wish you had what she had or you wish you were more like her.

It is a terrible feeling to think that somehow you aren't good enough just the way you are. If you catch yourself having jealous feelings toward another girl, ask yourself what it is about your life that you are unhappy with that makes you want to be like her.

How do you feel when you see another girl achieve something or get something really spectacular? Do you feel resentful? Instead of feeling jealous or thinking "Who does she think she is?", try to think how it would feel to be in her shoes. You must realize by now that accomplishments don't come easy. You know how hard you work for things that you have achieved. She must have worked hard, too!

Think of something you have achieved. Did you bring your grade up from a C to an A? Did you get accepted into the elite choir or band at your school? Did you win an award in sports? Accomplishments that make you feel proud require hard work, dedication and determination. Even if some achievements do come easy for you, you still have to put your time and energy into them.

Doesn't it feel good when someone congratulates you or pats you on the back for your effort? Remember that the next time you find feelings of jealousy creeping in on you. Choose to be a strong role model. Shake the other girl's hand, say congrats or good luck, and walk away feeling good about yourself and inspired by her—not jealous!

When you see another girl achieve, you can

applaud her efforts like you would hope others would do for you. Plus, seeing someone else accomplish something shows us what is possible. If she can do it, then we can, too, if we work hard enough. Another's accomplishments give us something to aspire to. Remember, if you think you want what she has, ask yourself if you are willing to do what she had to do to get it!

Jealousy between girls isn't always over each other's accomplishments. Jealousy rears its head over material things as well. We can feel jealous because another girl has a certain dress that we saw in a magazine, or because she got a new car when she turned 16.

You may wish for a car when you turn 16, but do you really wish you had that girl's life? Maybe she got the car because her dad works seven days a week and she never sees him, so he bought it for her out of his guilt. Or maybe her parents bought her the car to make her feel better because they recently divorced. In truth, she would rather have no car or an old beat-up car in exchange for a happier home life. Be careful what you wish for.

Jealousy toward someone is really a form of judgment. You make assumptions about the other person. You feel insecure or inadequate around her, so you try to knock down her enthusiasm. After all, "Who does she think she is?"

If you take the time to get to know the girl you're feeling jealous of, you might very well be surprised. She may turn out to be one of the nicest people you know! You may realize that, although she doesn't have the same problems you have, she struggles with problems of her own. You may find that she is much more deserving of her award or accomplishment than you could've imagined! Is it really that hard to give someone the same benefit of the doubt that you would hope to get?

Jealousy can be negative and destructive. If you find yourself having such feelings, choose to rethink the situation and act in a way that you can feel proud of.

Who Does She Think She Is?!?

◇◇◇◇◇◇

I would not be doing justice to the topic of relationships between girls if I did not talk about GOSSIP. Unfortunately, gossip is a frequent part of interaction between girls. We LOVE to talk! We talk about ourselves and, very often, we talk about other people.

Let's start with the definition of gossip. Gossip is idle conversation about others, regardless of fact. First of all, it is "idle conversation." It doesn't have much meaning, it is not going to solve any problems in the world, it is basically a waste of words and of time!

The second part, "regardless of fact," is critical when considering why gossip can be so damaging and why we should not take part in it. When we are gossiping about another person, we don't always know for sure that what we are saying is the actual truth. It's usually something we heard from some other source. Even if you think you know it is true, are you sure?

GRADUATING GIRLHOOD

Maybe you actually saw someone do something or heard someone say something. Let me ask you this: Do you know EVERYTHING that led up to that action or those words?

Have you ever been in a situation or said something that if someone saw or heard only part of it, they could make assumptions about you? If someone assumes the worse and starts spreading rumors about you, there's not much you can do about it. It is hurtful and frustrating. You can't go to every person who might have heard the gossip and explain yourself.

If a rumor was spreading about you like wildfire and it got to a girl named Suzy, wouldn't you appreciate it if she didn't spread it? What if Suzy thought "I don't know if it is true or not, and I don't want to participate in gossip, so I am not telling anyone else what I just heard." Wouldn't you feel thankful?

Next time you hear a rumor, why not try to be like Suzy? Be the person who doesn't add fuel to the gossip fire at someone else's expense. I'll bet people will respect you for that. And it is another quality you can feel proud of yourself about.

Although gossip is common among girls, we all know someone who is particularly "in the know" about everybody else's business! You know, the girl who has the scoop on everybody and everything! Consider for a moment if that is really someone you want to be around. If she is always telling you other people's secrets, what makes you think she's not turning around and telling other people yours? Is that the kind of person you want to put your trust in? You do not want to be a gossip, and you do not want to consider someone who is a gossip a true friend.

◇◇◇◇◇◇

Gossip can become a habit. It can end up being a big part of your communication with other girls, without you even realizing it. There are two ways to put an end to that and concern yourself with more important things:

1. Stop yourself and realize that you don't

know everything about that person or her circumstances. Maybe she wore the same shirt two days this week because her mom is in the hospital and her dad didn't have time to buy laundry soap because he's working two jobs.

2. Pay more attention to the words that come out of your mouth. Just like we discussed in chapter one with regard to your thoughts, to change them, you must first be aware of what they are. You may find that you do indeed gossip too much. Only when you start paying attention can you choose to stop yourself and talk about more positive things. If you try, you can find something nice to say about anybody! It will make you feel good, I promise!

Not gossiping doesn't mean you can't talk to your friends about observations that you have about other people. Stick to this rule, and you will be fine: Don't ever say anything about a person that you would not be willing to say to his or her face. If you think you would feel ashamed or you would want to deny it, don't say it!

Who Does She Think She Is?!?

◇◇◇◇◇◇

You will find that each school year you have opportunities to make new friends. As you are becoming more social in your teenage years, you may find that you want to redefine what makes a good friend for you. The qualities you look for in someone to hang out with and call your girlfriend may change, and some long-term friendships may grow apart. It is all a natural part of growing up.

As you gain more independence with your time, and have more of a social life, some friendships can take a turn for the worse. People you thought were your friends may not handle their newfound freedom well. You may have some friends who really struggle and want to defy authority and go on the wild side.

We will discuss peer pressure in chapter four, but don't feel bad if a friendship ends or if you cannot support a friend who is making choices that will hurt her. A true friend would not stand by and watch someone she cares about take risks that have negative consequences. A good friend would speak up. If that doesn't work, consider getting out of the relationship to protect yourself.

When you were younger, you may have been friends with a girl because she lived in your neighborhood. You were too young to drive, so it was easy. You may have chosen a friend because you were in Girl Scouts together. You shared that experience with her so you considered her a friend. Things like honesty, morals, common ideals or religious values weren't fully developed yet, nor were they considered important issues in the friendships you had before now.

As you grow to new levels of maturity and the stakes of friendship become higher, what's important in a friend may change. You are no longer just trading Barbie clothes or making up dance moves to your favorite songs. Now you want someone whom you can trust not to gossip about you, not to be jealous of you, to be happy for you when something good happens. You want a friend who will not ask you to lie or put you in uncomfortable situations on her behalf.

It is essential to have a friend who doesn't just talk all the time, but is willing to really listen. These are traits you will find to be important in a true friend. These are qualities we need when we talk about deep, long-lasting friendships, which we are lucky if we have more than one of.

◇◇◇◇◇◇

In addition to your circle of girlfriends, it is important to consider yourself in a kinship with all girls—you know, a sisterhood. People who don't fall into the perfect-match category are not by any means the enemy. It would be wonderful if we could try to look at every girl through eyes of kindness.

> *It would be wonderful if we could try to look at every girl through eyes of kindness.*

This is easier than you might think. Small acts of kindness along with making an effort to eliminate jealousy and gossip can dramatically alter the future of women's relationships for the better.

Would it be so difficult to smile at other girls? I realize you can't be close friends with EVERY girl in your school, but how about saying hello as you pass other girls in the hallway between classes? Or why not introduce yourself to the new girl? The golden rule applies here: Treat others the way you would like to be treated!

Let's embrace one another, our uniqueness and our differences of opinion, and realize the full potential of GIRL POWER! It is something we can only get from one another!

Who Does She Think She Is?!?

Affirmations

I live in harmony with other girls by
__being friendly to eachother and being kind too__.

I benefit from good relationships with other girls by
__helping eachother.__

~ 3 ~

Where Do Teenage Boys Come From?

Now let's move on to the good stuff, the really complicated subject of so much of our affection . . . boys! Have you heard the statement "Men are from Mars, women are from Venus"? Well, that may be true, but I think teenage boys are even farther away from teenage girls than that! So I like to say, "Teenage girls may be from Venus, but teenage boys are from Pluto!" That's about as far away from Venus as you can get!

Men and women will always have differences

between them, but during teenage years those differences are multiplied by 10. As a matter of fact, in many areas, it is hard to find any similarities at all!

Teenage boys are just wired differently than girls are. Their thought process is different, the chemicals in their brain are different, their motivation for making decisions is different.

These differences are something to think about as boys develop from just friends to more than just friends in your life. When you're daydreaming about that first kiss with him, or about spending time alone with him and wondering what it will be like, how close you will be, if he will love you, if he could be the love of your life—you know, all those romantic thoughts and feelings like you see on TV and in movies—remember, that's all it is . . . daydreaming!

I can assure you that when he's thinking about being alone with you, his thoughts are nothing like yours. Teenage boys are mostly thinking about experimenting and experiencing. They aren't thinking about the possibility of marrying you someday and loving you forever! This is just one more thing to add to your list of reasons not to have sex as a teenager. The expectation you have will not be fulfilled, no matter what he says to you.

The reality is that the emotional maturity and the responsibility required for a safe and meaningful sexual relationship are not present in our teenage years. All a sexual relationship can add to your life at this age is complications. Sex will mess with your emotions and compromise your self-esteem, not to mention the risks of pregnancy, disease and your reputation.

I have talked to many young women who are in college or in their 20s. The ones who gave in and had sex as teenagers tell me that they regret having done it. They ALL wish they would have waited. Not one of them who waited says she wishes she would have gone ahead and had sex back then, not one single person. Does that tell you something?

Now that we have established that sex is not a good option, let's talk about other issues that come up in dating relationships between guys and girls. One common tendency that girls have in their relationships with boys is to try to take care of them and try to solve their problems.

As women, we are natural caregivers. The problem is that many teen girls get so tangled up in their first real boyfriend that they do not think about the future. It is easy to get caught up in the idea of love and romance and lose sight of other things in your life. If you give boyfriends in middle school and high school all of your free time, all of your attention and all of your energy, many other areas of your life (school, friendships, family) will suffer.

If you think about the big picture of your life, you will realize that there's probably going to come a day when you'll get married and have a husband and household to care for. Then you may decide to have children whom you will be caring for. Many, many years of your adult life as a woman will most likely be spent caring for other people. Taking care of others may very well be your primary role.

Where Do Teenage Boys Come From?

It is important to understand that NOW is the time to take care of yourself! Teenage years and into your 20s are the time to be free of all of those obligations. It is the time to do things you enjoy; to try new things; to look forward to meeting new people in high school, in college and when you start your career. Now is the time to have a healthy balance in your life. Keep that journal, get to know who you are as a person, not just as somebody's girlfriend!

Picture yourself as a beautiful flower. At the center of the flower is your heart, your dreams, your spirit. The big petals that make up the flower represent your life. One petal is your education, one is your health, one is your hobbies, one is your family, one is your friends, and another might be your boyfriend.

Try to keep your flower petals balanced. Think about your life now. Are you spending time and energy in each area? Are you growing and enjoying many different things?

I bet you have known someone who gives up

most of her time with friends, family and other activities when she gets a boyfriend. He takes up all of her time. She doesn't call you as much. He seems to be the only thing that matters to her. Do you know someone who has done that? Hopefully it wasn't you. If it was, you've already learned this lesson the hard way!

What happens when that girl and boy break up? When things don't work out, it seems like the end of the world. The pain seems so much greater and it feels impossible to go on. If you didn't maintain balance, your friends may not be there for you, you may have alienated your parents, and your grades might be suffering. You've wrapped so much of yourself into that boy that the breakup feels 10 times worse than it really is. It is much harder to pick up the pieces and move on. It can really cause your self-esteem to plummet.

If you keep balance in your life, you can recognize a breakup as a learning experience. You can realize that the breakup is probably for the best and things will be all right. Most importantly, you'll know that YOU will be all right. You'll know that even without him, you are whole.

Having those kinds of healthy feelings after the many breakups and disappointments in life is something money can't buy you. A new outfit will not make you feel better. In order not to be devastated by every blow, you have to make the effort to have balance in your life. Balance is possible, but it takes effort. And that's something only you can do for yourself.

If you feel a strong need to nurture, you can volunteer for a local charity. Many organizations would benefit from your time and talent. If that doesn't fit your schedule right now, you can offer to walk a neighbor's dog. Dogs love attention, and they don't have the capacity to complicate your life!

◇◇◇◇◇◇

Another thing that is important for you to know, as you begin dating, is that you cannot change anyone.

For decades, we women have been getting

hooked on guys who either do not want to be with us or who treat us poorly. For some reason we rationalize it. We think he will change. We see his potential. We think we will be the one to change him. We tell ourselves things like "If I only love him enough, or sacrifice enough, he will finally see how much I care and he will love me back." Or something equally as irrational: "He has been my boyfriend for three months, and I know he has a good side. I'm not giving up now."

I want to tell you that if a guy is not treating you respectfully or in a way you think you deserve to be treated, tell him about it once. You may both be able to learn from that experience and move forward. But if he continues to treat you in any way less than you want to be treated, hear me now: HE IS NOT GOING TO CHANGE.

Picture a neon sign over his head that reads: "This is who I am right now, this is the way I want to be." This is the reality of the situation, this is how he is. Nothing you say or do after the first attempt will make things different. You can cross your fingers, wish upon a star, wear new perfume, or try harder, but whatever you choose, it will not change him.

Do yourself a favor. Cut your losses and move on. In business we call it the "sunk cost" theory. The advice of that theory is not to consider what you've already invested when trying to determine whether to continue with a relationship or project or whether to move on to a new one. There's no sense in wasting your time on someone who is not interested or who has "potential" to someday be more like the guy you're looking for! Count your blessings and know that you deserve the best and nothing less. If you don't believe this, neither will any guy you meet.

◇◇◇◇◇◇

We mentioned earlier a little bit about the romantic notions of spending time alone with a boy. But what can you expect when just going out, either with a group or as a couple? Dating can be a really fun and exciting time, packed full of fun activities like going to the movies, ice skating, concerts, and school dances! It is fun getting to know other people.

There are certain things about dating that are negotiable, like how much time to spend together each week or where to go on your dates.

Other aspects of dating are personal preferences. Do you want your date to open the door for you? Do you want your date to pay 100 percent of the time? These are issues that each girl will feel differently about. Some girls don't mind paying once in a while or splitting the cost of a date 50–50 most of the time. These are examples of personal preferences.

Some aspects of dating, however, are non-negotiable and are not subject to personal preference. There are some guidelines that apply to everyone.

First of all, it is NEVER acceptable for a date to be forceful with you. Grabbing or hitting in any way under any circumstances is unacceptable, as is any form of intimidation or control. You should feel safe and comfortable being yourself. You should be able to say no to anything you're not interested in doing or any place you're not willing to go.

A guy should never tell you who you can see, what you can or can't do, what you can or can't wear, who you can or can't call, or who your friends should be. At first this behavior can seem flattering: He is saying these things or acting jealous because he "cares" so much about you. But this kind of behavior is not a sign of how much a guy cares. It is not appropriate. In a healthy relationship, people act as partners. One person does not try to control the other's behavior.

Another rule is that if he respects you, he will respect your parents. Your parents have raised you and cared for you all these years, and you still live

> *If he respects you, he will respect your parents.*

under their roof. You owe them the respect of abiding by the rules they set for you in regard to your first years of dating. That includes how late he can call, what time you have to be home, and what events or activities are not acceptable at your age.

Any guy who tries to get you to break your parents' rules is bad news. If he doesn't respect them, he doesn't respect you. And what kind of a relationship are you going to have with a guy who lacks respect?

It is critical as you are forming dating relationships and forming your identity during these years that you pay attention to the relationships in your life. Don't fall victim to the many common mistakes of girls your age. Develop good, positive relationship skills now that will follow you through life and ultimately help you get the kind of marriage and family you want.

Where Do Teenage Boys Come From?

Affirmations

I deserve a relationship that is
kind, helpful, friendly and safe.

I keep balance in my life by
helping other people and people helping me.

~4~

Don't Go With the Flow!

Now you have some good ideas about what it is like and what it takes to have healthy relationships. You know that a good relationship with yourself is where all good relationships begin. Having a good relationship with yourself and having strong self-esteem, however, do not take away the desire to feel like you fit in with others.

It is normal to hope others will like you. We all have a basic need to feel accepted at some level. This desire is particularly strong during adolescence. Going through middle school and high school are your first major social experiences. You find yourself thrown into all kinds of situations with other teenagers: five to seven different classes in a day, the lunchroom, sports teams, school dances, and other extracurricular activities.

    The environment of school can feel like being in a fishbowl. Just like a fish swimming in a glass bowl can be seen by others from any angle, it feels like whatever you do, wear and say, someone is always watching—and judging you. So you worry: Do they like me? Do my clothes look all right? Is my hair OK? Does this sound familiar? You are not alone!

    These concerns are natural and come with the territory of being a teenager. You are no longer just your parents' kid. You are becoming an individual. And you're doing so in a very public place . . . school! The other kids are going through the same things you are and, although you may not be able to tell it, most of them have the same uncertain feelings.

Don't Go With the Flow!

The good news is that this is a temporary phase! Whether you fit in right now with the other kids in your school, or the other "fish" in your fishbowl, is no indication of your future success in life. Success in life will be measured in many different ways, but none of them will include whether you were the most popular girl in school, what brand of jeans you wore, whether you were asked to the prom, or whether you had a bad haircut!

As a matter of fact, after high school, you can choose to move on to an aquarium where the fish are more like yourself. As an adult, you will be free to swim in a huge ocean where there are so many different varieties of fish that your outward characteristics won't stand out at all!

Because this is a time when you're trying to find your identity and everyone around you is doing the same, who does what and who says what seem very important. Other people aren't paying as much attention to what you're wearing, what your hair looks like and what you're doing as you think they are. It feels that way sometimes, but most of the time these issues are a much bigger deal to us than to anyone else.

We all want to be liked by others, but as you are learning, you cannot please everyone. Even the most popular girl has someone or some people who do not like her!

Many things you are worrying about now will seem less important to you as you get older. I know it's hard to imagine, especially if you are in a fishbowl where you feel like you don't fit in with the other fish!

Most of the time you cannot control factors such as who likes you or dislikes you and for what reason. Because of that, it is important to keep perspective and know that your current level of popularity or unpopularity among your peers is no indication of the future success you will have in life! Your current peers probably will not be the ones hiring you or signing your paycheck!

Many star athletes and high-school beauties

end up struggling later in life when they find that the world outside of school is not as impressed with such qualities. The popularity that someone has in high school may not carry them far in the real world.

On the flip side are the ordinary students who end up doing extraordinary things in life. Oprah Winfrey and Bill Gates are examples. Both are very successful, very wealthy, doing what they love, and making a positive difference in our world. Ask them how popular they considered themselves in middle school or high school and they might laugh at you!

So, the next time you find yourself worrying about what others think about you, your clothes or your hair, focus instead on things that can and will make a positive difference in your future. Focus your attention on things like getting good grades, taking challenging classes, learning about areas of interest for a career, your health, sports, and developing good relationships with your family and friends.

The thing to remember is that how you feel

today is only temporary (I promise) and it will change many times in the next few years. So don't be too hard on yourself based on what others think. You never know what kind of beautiful and interesting fish you will end up being!

◇◇◇◇◇

Peer pressure is sometimes part of our quest to be popular. Our desire to fit in with a particular group might require us to behave in ways that we otherwise would not. In such cases, you may gain the acceptance you thought you were looking for, but at what price? If you do something against your beliefs just to fit in, you have given in to peer pressure.

We cannot leave the topic of girlfriends, boyfriends and popularity without talking about such pressures. We all know that peer pressure exists and we've all been told not to give in to it, but what is the best defense against peer pressure?

Sure, you can "just say no" and, of course, you can try to hang out with "good" people to minimize your chances of feeling negative pressure to do something that's not in your best interest. But the **best** defense against peer pressure is A GOOD RELATIONSHIP WITH YOURSELF!

When you've made the effort to spend time alone and keep a journal, you are less likely to act impulsively. When you have taken the time to know yourself and what you want for your life, you are

> *But the best defense against peer pressure is*
> *A GOOD RELATIONSHIP WITH YOURSELF!*

less likely to be persuaded to do things that will not help you get what you want. You will have more focus and determination.

If you have a good relationship with yourself, adults do not have to tell you things like "Don't do drugs." They do not have to tell you not to smoke cigarettes or not to have sex as a teenager. You will know those things. You will realize that risky behavior has negative consequences. You will not want to participate in anything that will work against you achieving your potential.

A good relationship with yourself can also help you handle peer pressure because when you have good self-esteem, you tend to attract positive people to your life. And there is a real benefit to being around people who have goals of their own and who respect yours.

✧✧✧✧✧✧

Sometimes when teens participate in something risky or illegal, their defense is that they didn't mean to or intend to, it "just happened," they were just "going with the flow."

That may sound reasonable or like something that could happen to anyone, right? So, what is the problem with "going with the flow"? The problem is that when you are out with your friends and you go with the flow of the actions of the group, you aren't making your own decisions. And if you think about it, for something to be flowing, it must be heading slightly downstream. This means that eventually you will end up somewhere below where you want to be.

Instead of being closer to your goals, you will find yourself wondering how you got so far off track. And to make matters worse, once you're in the flow of going with the actions and desires of others, it is very difficult to get out and paddle back upstream to where you really want to be. It's certainly much more difficult than if you take the time to build the relationship you have with yourself and make your own choices based on what is best for you!

Popularity and peer pressure are issues that all teens deal with. I want to encourage you to stand strong. Remind yourself that whether you're popular or not popular, that status is only temporary. And if you concentrate on all the things you can do to build a better future for yourself, negative peer pressure will not cause you to go astray. Just remember: DON'T GO WITH THE FLOW!

Affirmations

I am capable of making my own decisions. Doing so makes me feel

_____
_____.

I surround myself with people who are

_____
_____.

~5~

They Just Don't Understand!

Of all the primary relationships in your life, the relationships you have with your parents and other adults are important ones.

During teen years, your relationship with your parents (and some other adults who are part of your life) goes through an awkward time—awkward for you and awkward for them. Like other relationships you have, many things are changing and shifting during this time.

Even under the best circumstances—your parents are married to each other, supportive of you and pretty cool people—the relationship can feel strained. You can count on the fact that there will be times when you will feel severely misunderstood by your mom, your dad, or both. You probably won't like the way they treat you some days or some of the rules they impose on you.

As you make the transition from child to adult, you are yearning for independence and wanting to spread your wings. They are just trying to get used to the idea! Even good parents can struggle with the idea of their child growing up and with the changes they see taking place in you.

If you go into this phase knowing that it might be difficult at times, knowing that other kids are going through some of the same things, and knowing that this, too, shall pass, you will be able to cope better in times of frustration.

No matter how it feels at times, I can assure you that neither one of your parents wakes up in the morning and wonders, "How can I make my teenage daughter's life miserable today?"!

They Just Don't Understand!

◇◇◇◇◇◇

It is important to keep in mind that your parents (or whoever is raising you) are not perfect, and they are trying to learn how to deal with the more mature you! The grass is not necessarily greener on the other side. If you think your life would be perfect if only your mom were more like Caty's mom, or if only your dad were like Jill's dad, you are mistaken. You would just be trading in one set of struggles for different ones.

If you feel resentful because only one of your parents is raising you, you must realize that it is not easy for that one parent. Someday you will have a job, a home to take care of and bills to pay, and you will realize how hard a single parent has to work. As much as you would like some slack sometimes, why not cut some slack to the person who takes care of you the most, for not being perfect.

There are many kids who go to sleep every night wishing they had a mom or a dad to live with. Someone else is raising them. Think of the kids in foster care, think of the kids whose parents have died. Remember, there is ALWAYS someone better off and worse off than you are!

◇◇◇◇◇◇

As with any relationship, the only person you have control over is yourself. It is no different whether you're relating to parents, teachers, aunts, or any other adults. In those relationships, are you being the best YOU you can be? Take mental notes: Do you behave in a way that you feel proud of? Do you sometimes find yourself behaving ungratefully or disrespectfully when interacting with the adults around you?

If your relationship with an adult is making you feel misunderstood, frustrated or angry, and you would like it to be better, the place to begin to make it better is with yourself. Change your attitude the next time you interact and see if that makes a difference.

How can you change your attitude if you're *REALLY* mad? Here is something you can try: Write in your journal. Pour your negative emotions out on the pages, not to the person's face. At the bottom of your journal page, you can add three things that you are thankful to that parent/adult for. Being grateful always puts things in a better perspective, and it helps us behave in ways that are more true to who we really are and how we really want to be.

You can also spend some time thinking about the situation. Do you really have a reason to feel this way, or is it just a misunderstanding and you know deep down that they care for you and are just trying to do what's best? And don't forget: To have a more positive attitude, you can ALWAYS think of someone better off and someone worse off than you!

If there is just one specific issue that you and your parent can't agree on—like how late you can stay out—you may need to try a different approach: negotiation. Being able to negotiate is a skill that will benefit you often in life in all of your relationships. Here are some ideas on how to break the barrier on a specific problem.

GRADUATING GIRLHOOD

First, pick the appropriate time to bring the issue up. Rather than request a later curfew when you're on the phone with your girlfriend or when you're walking out the door, try bringing it (or whatever the issue is) up at a time when you're not pressuring them for an answer RIGHT NOW. Try, perhaps, when you're alone in the car with your parent or on a Saturday morning after breakfast.

When you put a person you're trying to negotiate with on the spot about the issue of disagreement, his or her defenses are high. And because it's something you want to go your way, your emotions are high. Both circumstances do not make for good negotiation!

Another good skill to use to smooth over a specific issue and make the situation better is *compromise*. Compromising does NOT mean you have to give in. It means coming up with a neutral solution that is more acceptable to both people involved. In the example we're using of trying to get a later curfew, compromise could work well. If being home at 9:00 p.m. is way too early for you, but being home at midnight is way too late and unacceptable to your parents, ask if they would be willing to compromise on 10:00 or 10:30. At least you get an extra hour with your friends, and at least they can expect you home at a reasonable hour so they don't have to worry.

The good thing about an arrangement like this is that if you keep your end of the bargain by getting home at the new time, you will establish trust. Once you prove that you are capable of acting responsibly, your parents may be more flexible in the future or on special occasions when you need it the most!

Ultimately if there is an issue between you and your parents that you cannot seem to resolve, you must realize that their rules are final. As long as you live in their house and they pay the bills, buy your clothes and feed you, you have to respect that they have the final say.

You may think they are wrong or just being

stubborn, but sometimes adults' years of experience allow them to see the bigger picture or potential problems that you cannot see. Very often when you look back later, you end up being thankful that you did not get your way and that your parents protected you.

Keep in mind that this is only temporary. You are not going to be a teenager needing your parents' permission forever. You have plenty of years

> *You are not going to be a teenager needing your parents' permission forever.*

ahead of you with your own freedom. Although that sounds GREAT right now, having to make all your own decisions will be tough at times. So don't be in such a rush for freedom and adulthood. Take it one step at a time!

◇◇◇◇◇

I know that some of you may have parents with a lot of problems who are not doing a very good job of raising you. Even if you feel that your parents are not supportive of you or that your relationship has not been good for years, there are other adults who do care about you.

Sometimes it is another relative who is part of your life who wants to see you succeed and be happy. Sometimes it is a teacher, a coach, a neighbor, a family friend, or a counselor. There are always adults in your life who want to see you grow into a happy and successful person. Take a moment to consider who these people are in your life.

You can create good relationships with those adults or improve existing relationships by recognizing who those people are who want to be there for you and then letting them into your life. You can nurture those key relationships by spending time with them and opening up with them about how things are going for you. Occasionally it is important to acknowledge them with a phone call or a note just to say "thank you." Let them know you appreciate them and the way they care. Not only will it make the person receiving the message feel good, it will make you feel good, too!

In conclusion, although the relationships you have with adults can seem frustrating at times, if you look, you can always find things to respect and cherish about the ones who care for you most. When things get tough, practice using the skills you learned in this chapter and remind yourself that it won't be this way forever! Good luck!

They Just Don't Understand!

Affirmations

Adults respond to me positively because

_____

_____.

I am thankful to my parents for

_____

_____.

~6~

"If Only My ___ Were ___ ."

    This chapter on body image falls between the relationship section and the goal-setting section of this book because it involves both. We all have a relationship with our body, and we all have goals of what we would like to change about it.

    As women, we especially tend to struggle with this relationship throughout our lives. As you are becoming more aware of your body and the changes that have been taking place, it is important to consider how to make this lifelong, intimate relationship a healthy one!

GRADUATING GIRLHOOD

As Americans, we are bombarded with visual images of thin, beautiful, "perfect" women. We see them in magazines, on billboards, on TV; it seems like they are everywhere we turn! We use the outward physical appearance of people to define what "beautiful" and "perfect" body types are. And from those images, we come to the conclusion that we do not measure up.

Your body image is the way you see yourself. It is the way you feel about your physical appearance. We've all known a very slim girl who is constantly talking about how "fat" she is. And we've all known an athletic, muscular, full-figured girl who feels just great about her body. It is really a matter of self-perception, which begins in our thoughts.

Your body is an impressive machine. If you get the chance to take a human anatomy class, you should. You would be amazed by all the things that take place 24/7 inside of you to keep you alive and healthy. Yet, instead of being respectful of this miracle, for decades women have found ways to disrupt

"If Only My _____ Were _____."

the natural system of their bodies in an attempt to change their outward appearance.

Instead of giving it what it wants and needs, some women try to change their body by taking diet pills or going on unhealthy diets like eating ONLY fruit or ONLY protein. Some women starve themselves, eat only once a day, or throw up after meals. Many women even take the serious measure of going under the knife to have plastic surgery. All surgery is serious and has risks of side effects. Just because breast implants, liposuction and nose jobs are optional surgeries does not make them 100 percent safe!

◇◇◇◇◇◇

The first step to take to improve our relationship with our physical bodies is to pay attention to and improve our thoughts. As we discussed in chapter one, we talk to ourselves with our thoughts all the time.

If you want a good body image, you have got to notice what kind of things you say to yourself about your body. Are you often thinking negative things like "I am too short and my hips are too wide"? Or like this chapter title says, "If only my _____ were _____." It is only when you begin to notice those thoughts that you can change them.

You don't have to lie to yourself or be in denial, but for every negative thing you think, if you try, you can come up with something to feel good about. Just like other areas in your life, there is ALWAYS someone better off and someone worse off than you are. There are many girls who would love to have the physical feature you complain about most.

Every time you catch yourself saying you don't like something about a physical feature of yours, consciously think of something you really do like about yourself. Do you have beautiful hair? Do you have strong, muscular legs? If you are thankful for all the functions your body allows you to perform every day, your body image will easily improve.

Everybody, and I mean EVERYBODY, has

"If Only My ___ Were ___ ."

things that they would like to change about their body if they could—even supermodels. I once heard a famous supermodel say her lips are too crooked, and her hips are too wide!

Did you know that the models we see on magazine covers do not even look that perfect in real life? Magazine publishers have all kinds of ways to alter photographs with computer technology. They can make teeth whiter, legs thinner <u>and</u> longer, breasts larger; remove pimples; decrease waist size; and the list goes on! You name it, they can change it. It is so deceptive. The images we compare ourselves to and envy and try to live up to are not even real!

It's no wonder so many girls and women feel inadequate about their bodies! This is very sad because your body is the vehicle God has given you to get through life. I encourage you to take care of it . . . it is the only one you will have!

◇◇◇◇◇◇

As you get older, you will realize that your identity and your value are not tied up in how you look. Your physical appearance is just part of the equation. Your mind, your sense of humor, your generosity, and your commitments to others all influence how other people see you. Outward beauty is only skin deep. Being physically beautiful does not make you a good person or better than anyone else.

As with all areas of your life, what you can expect from your physical body is not perfection, but for it to be the best it can be. This involves many things. The key components that contribute to a healthy relationship with your body are your thoughts, exercise, nutrition, and avoiding obvious negative influences. Do what you can to have a healthy body, not to achieve a certain weight on the scale.

◇◇◇◇◇◇

Exercise is probably the most important habit you can develop. The obesity rate among Americans and among people your age is rising at an alarming rate. There are just so many things calling for your time that do not involve physical activity. It

"If Only My _____ Were _____ ."

is possible to go for a week or a month without exercising and not even notice! You can be entertained by TV for hours with some 50 to 300 channels. You can easily spend an entire evening surfing the Net or playing video games. And, of course, one of our favorite pastimes: Talking on the phone doesn't require any exercise, either!

If you're involved in sports, it is no problem to get exercise every week. If you're not, consider signing up for more PE classes or look for an activity that you enjoy. You can go for a walk, buy an exercise video, join a sports team or a class at the YMCA. Invite a girlfriend over, turn up your favorite music and dance for 30 minutes!

There are many ways to get exercise and it is very important. Even if you have a disability, ask your doctor or physical therapist to give you exercises that will help you feel stronger!

Exercise helps you stay in shape, it increases your endurance, relieves stress, helps your body function properly, and it can be fun! Regular exercise can improve your body image in two ways. When you exercise, your brain releases endorphins, which are also known as "feel good" chemicals. So after a good workout, you have a sense of well-being. Also, as you increase your ability and performance in your activity or sport, you gain a new respect for your body and what it allows you to do! Respecting your body improves your body image instantly!

> *Respecting your body improves your body image instantly!*

If you are not exercising regularly (at least three times per week), figure out a way to make it part of your life. Think of something you used to enjoy when you were younger, or try something new. But like the Nike ad says, "JUST DO IT"![tm]

Nutrition is another important consideration in your relationship with your body. Food is fuel for your body. Taking care of your body means you feed it the fuel it needs and can use to give you energy. If weight isn't an issue, you may think you can eat whatever you like. Keep in mind that you are developing habits that will be very tough to break in the future.

You probably learned the food groups and basic nutrition in health class. Some additional key nutrition points for you to consider in establishing a healthy relationship with your body are:

1. Breakfast. Starting your day with food is VERY important. You may think you will lose or keep off extra weight by skipping it, but it has been scientifically proven that not eating breakfast will slow your metabolism for the day. Skipping breakfast puts your body in starvation mode. Not to mention the lack of energy and concentration you feel, and the tendency to overeat at lunch because you are starving! You would not try to start a car without gas, so why expect your body to start moving for the day without its fuel?

2. Variety. Your body will reward you by helping you feel and function your best when you give it a variety of foods. If you have the exact same meal for lunch every day, you are probably missing out on some important nutrients. We all know that eating fruits and vegetables is good for us. Add them into your day, and try to eat a balance of foods from the basic food groups.

3. Sugar. Another nutrition item to take into account is sugar. Sugar can wreak havoc on your system, your energy and your mood. If you haven't thought about it before, you might not even realize how much sugar you consume.

Sugar is in many food items. Of course there are the obvious ones like cake, ice cream and other desserts. But what about soda? Do you often drink soda? There are eight to ten teaspoons of sugar in one can of soda! Next time you open a can or bottle, picture yourself swallowing all those teaspoons of pure sugar! Maybe then you will switch out that soda for water or tea instead.

"If Only My _____ Were _____ ."

Sugar occurs naturally in fruits. Although it is a natural form, remember when determining your sugar intake that the fruit you eat and the fruit juice you drink do contain some sugar.

Although sugar is not bad for you, getting too much on a regular basis can be. Your body can get used to unhealthy surges of insulin, and you can gain excess weight. Sugar can affect your mood and ability to concentrate. Start paying attention to how much sugar you put into your body and make adjustments if you realize it is too much. Decreasing your daily sugar intake can really make you feel better.

4. Water. Water is another part of the equation for a healthy body. Water is a very essential nutrient that is often overlooked. Your body relies on water to perform many important functions within your cells. You need six to eight glasses of water each day.

How much water do you drink every day? If you don't think you are getting enough, have a glass in the morning while you get ready for school. Have a glass as soon as you get home. And have water with your meals.

I have touched on a few essential points here, but there are books and books on nutrition. If you feel that your health class does not answer all of your questions, go to the library and check out a book on the subject. It is your body and *you* are responsible for taking care of it. Develop good habits now and your body will reward you for it as you get older.

If you are trapped in an unhealthy habit of using extreme nutrition-depriving actions such as not eating hardly at all (anorexia) or eating in binges and then throwing up (bulimia), please reach out to someone for help. There are hotlines you can call in most cities, or your school counselor or nurse can probably lead you to an organization that can help. These kinds of behaviors are addictive and do not just go away.

An eating disorder is not something you will

"If Only My _____ Were _____ ."

just grow out of. It will probably get worse. If you or someone you know is struggling with these issues, get help right away: the sooner, the better.

The final proactive thing you can do to improve your body image is to avoid obvious negative influences. Some pitfalls that are proven to very negatively affect your relationship with your body are tobacco, alcohol and drugs. All three of these substances affect the chemistry of the brain and impair the body's ability to feel good naturally. If you are willing to put such harmful substances into your body, you cannot have a healthy body image. Not to mention all the negative things you know about them and that they are illegal for you to use.

Other less obvious pitfalls you can avoid are things like getting sunburn (use sunscreen) and not getting enough sleep (you need at least eight hours a night).

A healthy body image develops when you take care of yourself and monitor your thoughts about your body. You will never live up to some external level of perfection. If you start trying to achieve an impossible weight or size in order to feel OK about yourself, you are in for a lifelong struggle! We each have an obligation—not to have a perfect body, but to take care of the one we have!

Be the healthiest you can be, be grateful for the body you have been given, and you will be one step ahead on the road to happiness!

"If Only My _____ Were _____ ."

Affirmations

I love my body because

_____

_____.

I nurture my body by

_____

_____.

Setting

And

Achieving

Your

Goals

~7~

If You Aim at Nothing, You'll Hit It Every Time!

Incorporating the principles we covered in the first six chapters will go a long way in making your relationships healthy, supportive and meaningful. Those concepts alone, however, will not make your career or other life ambitions a reality. In this chapter, we will prepare you even more for graduating girlhood as we begin the discussion of another life-enhancing practice: setting goals.

People who are really successful in life have this one thing in common. They know that success is NOT about being lucky! Successful people figure out what it is they want, and then they figure out what they have to do to achieve it. It doesn't matter if the success they are seeking is in sports, business, finance or any other area . . . they all set goals. A goal is something you would like to have, something you would like to achieve. It is what you are willing to work for.

When you hear about goals, you hear words like "destination," "mission," "objective," "target." Setting goals is where all success begins. I love the saying "If you aim at nothing, you'll hit it every time!" If you do not give yourself something to aim for, how will you know when you miss the mark? How will you know when your hard work has paid off or when you've achieved something you can feel proud of?

Having clear goals helps you take charge of your life. Getting a date to the next school dance may be one of your goals. That would be a short-term goal, but now is the time to start thinking about

If You Aim at Nothing, You'll Hit It Every Time!

the bigger picture. Think about what you would like to achieve in the long term.

> *Having clear goals helps you take charge of your life.*

Your teenage years are the perfect time to begin this process! You are making all kinds of important decisions. Having clear goals will put you in charge of your future instead of waiting to see what comes along. Having goals will help you stay on track. Unfortunately, goal setting, like relationship skills, is not offered as a class in school.

◇◇◇◇◇◇

A critical component to set goals effectively is to know what you want. There are many considerations and people influencing you right now. It is especially important to make the effort not to go with what everyone else wants for you. Just because your best friend wants to go to beauty school doesn't mean you would enjoy that. Or just because your older brother went out of state to a big college doesn't mean that is the appropriate route for you. What do YOU dream of being or doing?

If you are like many other girls your age, you honestly don't know the answer to that question. A good place to begin the process or to expand your existing goals is, like we discussed in chapter one, to spend some time alone thinking about it.

An important part of figuring out what you want for your future and what your goals should be is to define what your strengths, your weaknesses and your interests are.

Define your personal strengths. Part of being human is that we all have strengths and we all have weaknesses. Some things come naturally to us, and some things are a struggle for us. It is different for every person. You were born with gifts and talents, and you owe it to yourself to figure out what they are and to explore them.

Are you comfortable meeting new people? Are you good at math? Does science fascinate you?

If You Aim at Nothing, You'll Hit It Every Time!

If you come up with things that you are good at, or that interest you, then you can go from there.

Let's say you love animals. How do you set a goal based on that? Well, you can start by educating yourself. Go to the library, get on the Internet, find out what kinds of careers you can have working with animals. Once you get some concrete ideas, talk to people. Find out from people who are already working with animals how they like it. What kind of education does it take? How much money can you expect to make? What is the best part of their profession? What is the biggest downfall?

Information is POWER! Just by educating yourself, you can come up with possibilities that you didn't even know existed! You may even rule out some options because, when you learn more, you may realize that they involve different things than you expected.

Next, define your weaknesses. Identify areas where you are uncomfortable or lack ability. Realizing what types of things you are not particularly good at is important. It would be unrealistic to say you want to be a congresswoman because you want to make a difference in your community, if you absolutely do not like to talk in front of people! Or by acknowledging that as a weakness, you can work extra hard to overcome it. Part of the goals you set can then include taking every public-speaking class you can. Or you can practice public speaking by joining a school organization that would require you to get up in front of a crowd and talk!

Your goals will be more appropriate for you and will have a better chance of being reached if you don't overlook your strengths and your weaknesses in the development process.

Goal setting is not a one-time event. Setting goals should be part of your lifelong development. Some of your goals may change with time. Instead of becoming a doctor, like your original goal was, you may realize two years into college that you really want to be a pediatric nurse. You may reach some goals and then set new ones. You may have

If You Aim at Nothing, You'll Hit It Every Time!

a goal to make the track team. Then, once you are on the team, you may set another goal to beat the school record in the 100-yard dash! The most crucial thing, though, is that you give it some thought and then give yourself something to shoot for, because *"If you aim at nothing, you will hit it every time!"*

◇◇◇◇◇◇

When you think about setting goals for your future, you probably think about your career or your profession. But goal setting is important for all areas of your life. Goals are appropriate for any area that you want to succeed in. You can have school-related or academic goals, physical goals and relationship goals. Following are examples of goals for these different areas of your life.

AREA OF LIFE	**EXAMPLE OF GOAL**
School/academic	Raise my Spanish grade to an A.
	Try out for and make the cheerleading squad.

AREA OF LIFE	**EXAMPLE OF GOAL**
Physical	Cut back on sugar—don't drink soda with dinner.
	Get exercise three times per week.
Relationships	Be more patient with my little brother.
	Speak more respectfully to my mom.
Career	Research three different careers this summer.
	Take challenging classes that will prepare me for college.
Personal	Spend at least one hour of quiet time alone every weekend.
	Find a local charity to raise money for or donate my time to.

I hope you are beginning to see why goal setting is so important and how having clear goals gives you direction to strive for the things you really want for yourself. Goals give you something to

If You Aim at Nothing, You'll Hit It Every Time!

shoot for. The process of determining your goals makes you take the time to identify what you want and where you are going. It is not too early to begin.

Goals can also be used as a measuring tool. You can look back and see how far you've come, which ones need more work to be achieved, or which ones need to be updated and changed.

Some people think that going through the process of identifying goals and figuring out how to make them happen is just too much trouble. "I'll just go with the flow," they say, or "I'll worry about that stuff later." It is your choice. You have the freedom to do or not do whatever you want. But the reality is that no one is going to do this for you. If you compare two girls who are 18 and one has been setting and working toward goals since she was 13 or 14 and the other has not, which girl do you think will be more successful? Which girl do you think feels better about herself and more confident about her potential? You decide which girl you are going to be.

Now that we have established that goal setting is important, the next chapter will provide the details you need to make your goal setting as effective as possible and help you succeed at the goals you set!

Affirmations

I give myself something to aim for because

_____
_____.

The time it takes to determine my goals is a worthwhile investment for me because

_____
_____.

~8~

If You're Really Lucky, You Will Be Successful . . . NOT!

Successfully setting and reaching goals is a skill. Such achievement is not about chance or being lucky! You are lucky if you win the lottery. You and all the other people who play do the exact same thing: You pay $1 for a ticket and then let chance determine who wins. The qualities required to reach your goals—hard work, determination and focus—do not equal luck!

Sometimes long-term goals or big dreams that you have for your future can seem impossible or overwhelming. There are some very specific things you can do to maximize your potential to achieve the goals you set for yourself.

In this chapter, we will examine seven key elements for effectively setting your goals and determining the course that will best help you reach them. Incorporating these elements will increase your likelihood of becoming the person you want to be and living the life you want to live!

First, *be as specific as possible.* For example, it is not helpful to say, "I want to do something in the medical field." You can't expect to know where to go from there. You can begin with that, but then you must research and make the effort to be more specific. Do you want to be a nurse? A doctor? A physical therapist? A medical transcriptionist?

Another example of a statement that is too general would be "I want to be healthier." In what way do you want to be healthier? How will you determine when you reach that goal of "being healthier"? Do you mean that you want to increase your cardiovascular endurance from being able to run one mile to being able to run two? Do you mean that you want to eat four small meals per day instead of one large one? Being as specific as possible with the statement of your goals will help you determine how to reach them.

Next, **be reasonable.** You do not want to limit yourself or your dreams for your future, but it is important to be realistic. If you are 5 feet 1 inch tall, for example, playing professional basketball is probably not a realistic goal. Perhaps you can be part of professional basketball in another way. You could become a physical therapist that specializes in sports-related injuries. You could get your journalism degree and become a sports writer or commentator.

Another example of a goal that is not reasonable is to raise your math grade from a D to an A by the end of the week! You want to be reasonable with the goals you set and how much time you give yourself to achieve them. I don't want to discourage you from aiming high for yourself, but I also don't want you to set yourself up for failure, only to be disappointed.

Once you have set a specific, reasonable goal, then you can **identify the necessary steps to achieve it.** This is where you gather as much information as you can. If it is a fitness goal you have, go to the library and read books to find out what fitness experts say you need to do. You can talk to your PE instructor or one of the team coaches at your school for advice. The Internet may also be an excellent source for information.

If your goal is a professional one, research what kind of education it will require. What classes do you need to start taking now?

Sometimes it helps to work backward from your goal to identify the steps. If you want to be a music teacher, you will have to get a teaching certificate before you get the job. Before you can apply for the certificate, you will have to get a college degree in music education. Before you can get that degree, you will have to determine which colleges

If You're Really Lucky, You Will Be Successful . . . NOT!

offer good music programs and how you will finance your education. Before you do that, you need to learn to play several instruments. Thinking backward from whatever goal you have requires you to identify the steps to achieve it. Eventually you realize what your first step forward should be. In this example, you would know to begin by taking extra music classes or private music lessons and researching various college music programs.

Do you see how the process works? Whatever method you use, you must take the time to identify the steps necessary to help you achieve your goals. This becomes your plan of action. Determining your plan of action takes luck out of the equation and puts you in the driver's seat of your future . . . starting TODAY!

> *Determining your plan of action takes luck out of the equation . . .*

The next step is to **give yourself a time**

frame to shoot for. It is one thing to say, "Someday I want to _____." It is quite another to say that by a certain date, or particular age, you will achieve it! You may very well have good intentions to someday achieve that something. But giving yourself a date or a time frame to aim for may make you more determined to get started and help you stay focused. Even if your time frame changes, it is important to have one in mind as you lay out your plans.

Now that you have a goal, a plan, and a time by which you want to achieve that goal, the next part of the process is to ***identify potential obstacles.*** It is realistic to realize that any goal you set will probably have obstacles to overcome.

If a college education is part of your plan, coming up with the money for tuition may be a very real obstacle for you. By realizing that now, you can begin thinking about your options so you may have the problem solved before it has a chance to hinder your progress.

If You're Really Lucky, You Will Be Successful . . . NOT!

For example, financial means for college may be available in many different ways. You may earn a scholarship, or you may apply for financial aid in the form of a grant or a low-interest loan. You may join the military, where you can get the training you need, or sign up for a specific military program that offers to pay for college after you have completed your time. You may look for a job with a company that will pay for you to get your education at night while working there during the day.

There are many ways. As with other issues that may come up, you can get creative to overcome or deal with obstacles that will otherwise hinder your progress. Like the saying goes, "Where there is a will, there is a way!"

◇◇◇◇◇◇

A common obstacle for many goals and dreams is fear. Fear is natural. Anytime you are trying to get beyond where you are, you aren't exactly sure what to expect, so it is not uncommon to experience some anxiety, doubt or fear. Fear can leave you frozen and unable to move forward to pursue your dreams—the fear of letting yourself down, the fear of letting your family down, the fear of failure.

When you're having these feelings of uncertainty, if you wait for someone to come along and encourage you or reassure you that you can reach your dreams, you may wait your entire life. You have everything you need to be successful. If it is a goal you are meant to achieve, you will. Just be smart about it and learn to trust yourself!

The next important step is to **put your goals in writing.** Keep your written goals in a place where you can see and reread them often. If you have a fitness goal, place the written goal in your gym bag.

Writing things down somehow makes them more permanent. Your goals seem more real when you can actually see the words. You can write your goals as affirmations. Like the affirmations at the end of each chapter, say your goals in positive statements. "I can run two miles with ease." "I am a thriving student at (college of your choice)."

If You're Really Lucky, You Will Be Successful . . . NOT!

The final recommendation I can give you to help increase the likelihood of reaching your goals is to **visualize your success.**

Your mind is a very powerful tool, so why not make it work in your favor? There is research that suggests that the mind does not differentiate between what is real and what is imagined. That's probably why you can feel your body relax when you close your eyes and imagine being on a peaceful, warm beach.

You can use this technique to help you reach your goals. Close your eyes every now and then and visualize what it will feel like to reach your goal. Try to imagine it in detail. Imagine yourself progressing through the steps of your action plan with ease.

You can use visualization daily before you go to sleep at night. If you plan to work out after school, imagine yourself getting out of your last class and feeling energetic. Visualize the exercises you will do. Imagine yourself feeling strong. This process

GRADUATING GIRLHOOD

can give you a clear mental picture of yourself reaching your goals and can set you up for success!

◇◇◇◇◇◇

You will find it helpful to re-evaluate these seven elements and your progress periodically. As you change and your circumstances change and as you grow toward your goals, you may need to make adjustments to your plan. Re-evaluating also helps to remind you of what your goals are and make sure you are on track.

Pick a time at least once per year to go over the goals you've set for yourself and to review the seven elements to see if any adjustments need to be made. Perhaps each year on your birthday, on New Year's Day, or on the first day of summer, you can sit down and re-evaluate. Whenever you choose, just make sure you do continue the process.

If you re-evaluate and find you are not at all closer to a particular goal, you may need to take an honest look at the possible reasons why. If you have a fitness goal, for example, and one of the steps to

If You're Really Lucky, You Will Be Successful . . . NOT!

reach that goal includes working out three mornings per week before school, and you are not keeping that commitment, you have to determine why. Is it due to lack of desire (you don't REALLY want the goal)? Or can it be achieved by another means? Maybe getting out of bed at 6:00 a.m. is incredibly difficult for you, but after school you have tons of energy!

You have to learn what will work for you. It's part of the process. If the goals you set for yourself or the steps to reach your goals conflict with your personality, it will be a constant struggle.

I hope it is clear to you that there are very specific things you can do (beginning now) that will put you on the path you want to be on. You do not have to wait until you are in college or for a guy to come along or for your horoscope to tell you it is OK, and it won't help to cross your fingers! Remember, success is NOT about being lucky! You just have to decide that you are capable of determining what you want out of life and figuring out how to get from where you are to where you want to be!

Affirmations

My destiny is not in the hands of "chance." I will succeed because

_____

_____.

Everything I need to achieve my dreams is within my reach.

~9~

GIRL POWER!

I am so happy and proud of you for reading to this point of GRADUATING GIRLHOOD! I hope you have found it useful and packed full of valuable information. And, of course, it is my dream that by reading the previous eight chapters, you have gained confidence as you are moving through the process of graduating girlhood!

In relationships, you now know the most fundamental truth: The quality of all relationships that you have stems from the relationship you have with yourself. How good or bad you feel about and treat

GRADUATING GIRLHOOD

yourself will directly influence all other relationships in your life.

In regard to your future, you now know that by setting goals for yourself, you do indeed possess GIRL POWER! With the choices that you make, you have the power to steer your life in the direction you want and achieve anything you set your mind to!

The topics we covered in this book are meant to add fuel to the fire of your life: to give you inspiration and expand your horizons. I want you to realize that you CAN have the life you want. I want you

> *You CAN have the life you want.*

to wake up 10 and 20 years from now and feel good about what you have done and where you are.

◇◇◇◇◇◇

You have a long life ahead of you. Even if you take my advice and make good choices and put your best foot forward, there will be ups and downs. Using the knowledge provided here will just help you along the way and make your journey less difficult; it will not take away all stress and disappointments. Ups and downs are just a part of life.

Don't let a failure discourage you. Failure is proof that you are taking chances and making the effort to live your dreams. Learn from your mistakes and misjudgments and continue to move forward. There is ALWAYS either an important lesson for you to learn from the experience OR there is a better path for you. As one door closes, another opens.

Remember, *"To every thing there is a season, and a time to every purpose under the heaven."* (Ecclesiastes 3:1)

You will enjoy your journey, if you understand that happiness isn't someplace you arrive. You will feel happy as you reach each of your goals, but that won't make you happy forever. Don't fool yourself with the idea that when you graduate, when you turn 21, when you get married, THEN you will be happy.

If you think happiness is a destination, it will forever elude you. My advice: Learn to enjoy the process. It is not an easy thing to do but something to keep in mind. Most of your life will be experienced during the PROCESS and trials of getting to each milestone.

Celebrate the happy times. In bad times, remember that they won't last forever. Adversity makes us stronger. Bad times give us a measure to appreciate the good times. If it never rained, how could we fully appreciate the beautiful sunny days?

When you're trying to make a decision, remember that the best choice is usually NOT the easiest. And if you still can't decide what to do, think of it this way: If it would not be what you would want your little sister to do, or if it wouldn't be a good decision for your future daughter, it is not the right choice for you, either!

Many young women don't understand how much power they really have to develop and change their lives and achieve their dreams. I don't want you to be one of those women! If I could, right now, I would put my hands on your shoulders, look you

GIRL POWER!

straight in your eyes and tell you how special you are. YOU are VERY special. Believe in yourself like I believe in you!

It is my desire that you apply the principles you've learned in this book. Pass GRADUATING GIRLHOOD on to a little sister or a friend, or keep it for yourself to review and give one as a gift to a friend. Let's add new excitement, knowledge and meaning to the process of GRADUATING GIRLHOOD!

Affirmations
I am a very special person!
I enjoy the process of graduating girlhood and look forward to becoming the woman I know I can be!

_____
_____
_____
_____
_____
_____.

About the Author

Denise Evans, speaker and author, founded Life-Enhancing Seminars in 1999. Her empowering presentations for adults and teens are designed to inspire participants to aim high and take charge of their lives! Her passion and commitment are especially evident in her work with teen girls—from girls-at-risk to emerging leaders.

Denise lives in Kansas City, Missouri with her husband and two furry, four-legged "kids," DJ and Maltee.

Contact Information:

Denise Evans
Life-Enhancing Seminars
P.O. Box 681427
Riverside, MO 64168

deniseevans@kc.rr.com

Give the Gift of

GRADUATING GIRLHOOD
A Teenage Girl's Guide to Success in Relationships & Life

Contact your local Bookstore or
shop Amazon.com.

To Purchase a personalized copy
Signed by the author:

Send a check or money order for $15.95*
*(11.95 + 4.00 shipping/handling)
*MO residents send $16.75 to include sales tax
To:
Life-Enhancing Publishing
P.O. Box 681427
Riverside, MO 64168
(Please include the name you want your book endorsed to!)

Or visit
www.graduatinggirlhood.com

For credit card orders
Call:
800-266-5564

Discounts available on orders of 25 or more.